Water Worlds

Jane Wood

Ginn

Water Worlds

In this book, you will learn about some of the extraordinary creatures that live in the sea. But be warned – these are no ordinary fish! These creatures are really amazing, and we are only just beginning to learn about them now. In fact, some scientists think we know more about outer space than we do about life in the deepest parts of the sea on our own planet! Are you ready to explore exciting underwater worlds for yourself?

As you dive to the bottom of the sea, write down and keep your answers to each **QUIZ** question. (Remember, the answers are in the book!) Ready? Get fishing!

New ways of exploring underwater are always being invented, and there's still a lot to learn about life under the sea.

Let's Go Fishing!

Deep, Hot and Smelly

What kind of sea creature lives in the hottest environment any animal can stand?

PAGES **6** TO **11**

What's in a Name?

Some names are just so confusing. Explore some of the strangest names under the sea!

PAGES **12** TO **13**

Cold Seas

How can any sea creature live in water that's colder than ice?

PAGES 14 TO 17

Eye Spy!

This sea creature can see in the dark!

PAGES 18 TO 19

Flashy Fish!

Which sea creature lives in the deepest, darkest parts of the ocean?

PAGES 20 TO 25

Sunny Waters

Which sea creatures laze in the sun and never go anywhere?

PAGES 26 TO 31

Deep, Hot and Smelly

Deep inside the earth, there is a hot core of burning rocks. Water seeps down towards this hot core through cracks in the ocean floor. The rocks heat this water and squirt it back up into the ocean in powerful, scalding hot jets.

In some places, the jets of hot water contain chemicals, which form solid black chimneys called 'black-smokers'. Most black-smokers are found more than a mile below the surface of the sea.

Foul Smelling Fact

The hot jets of water contain a chemical called hydrogen sulphide. This is the chemical used in stink bombs. It smells like rotten eggs!

On land, water usually boils at 100°C, but these super-heated jets of water can reach 400°C!

The hot jets of water gush up into the cold sea water, and the hot and cold water mix together. This makes an area of warm water, which is about 40°C in temperature. That's about as hot as a hot bath. Some creatures, like zoarcid fish, shrimps, clams and tubeworms live in this hot bath, right next to the scalding jets.

> Creatures that live in extreme conditions, like tubeworms, are called extremophiles.

Tubeworms are very odd creatures. They have a tough tube, which protects them like a shell. They have no mouth and no stomach, so they can't eat. They live on sugars produced by bacteria that live inside them! This unusual way of feeding obviously works well – tubeworms can grow to be two metres long!

Fact File

Name
Pompeii worm

Size
10 centimetres long

Appearance
Long and thin. They seem to be covered in fluffy grey wool, which is actually a coat of bacteria! They have red gills on their heads.

Home
Next to scalding hot water jets on the ocean floor, about 1.5 miles below the surface of the sea.

Food
They catch particles in the water using their red gills.

QUIZ Hydrogen ******** smells like rotten eggs

Pompeii worms can stand to live in hotter conditions than any other animal on earth! No one is sure how they manage it, but scientists believe that their coat of bacteria might help. Pompeii worms keep their gills in water that would feel warm to a human (22°C), but they put their back end into water that's nearly four times hotter, at 80°C! That's nearly as hot as boiling water!

The hottest water a Pompeii worm has ever been found in was 105°C – that's hotter than boiling water!

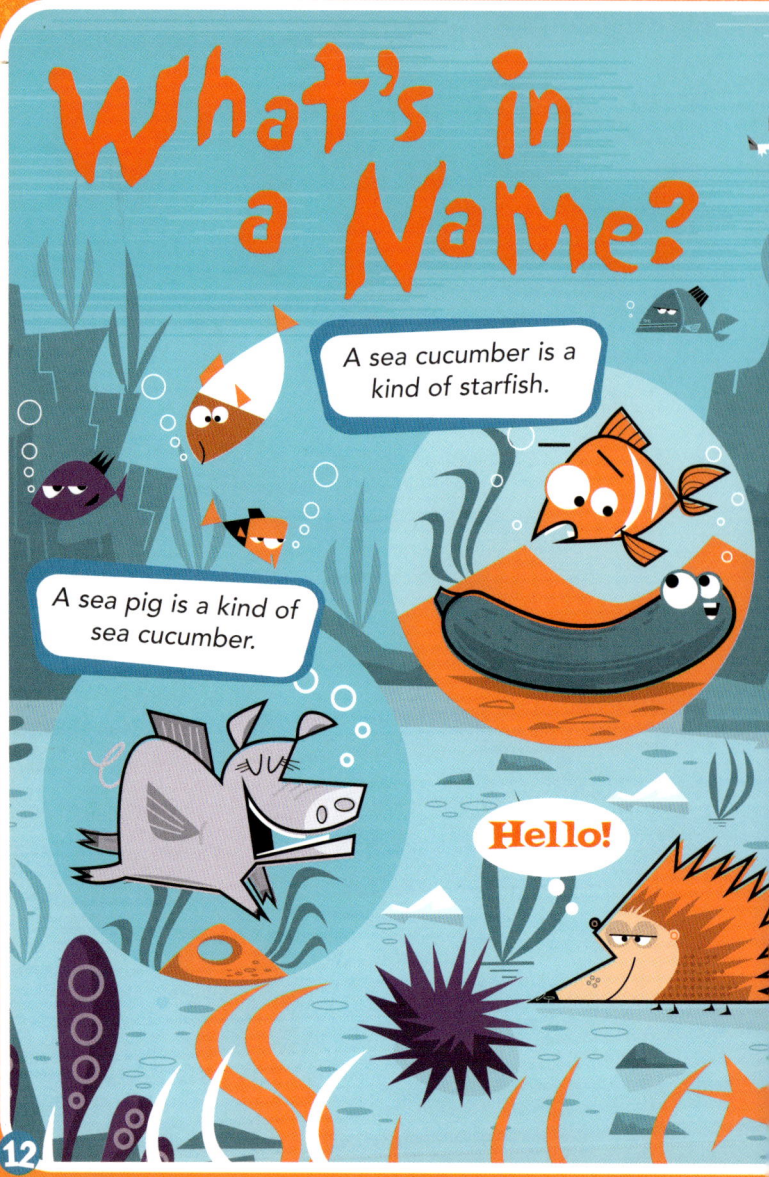

Cold Seas

The Arctic is an enormous frozen wilderness. The air temperature can reach −30°C. That's colder than a freezer … Brrrr! The ground is always frozen, and the sea is usually covered with ice.

Water on land usually freezes into ice at 0 °C. Sea water contains a lot of salt, and this changes its freezing point. It can get as cold as −1.9 °C before it freezes. But how can fish live in sub-zero temperatures? Why don't they freeze to death?

> Luckily I only have frozen fish fingers.

Well, fish make a special chemical, which acts like antifreeze in their bodies! The antifreeze works by attaching itself to any small ice crystals in the fish's body. It prevents any more ice crystals from joining on. So the ice can't grow any more, and the fish doesn't get completely frozen.

Fact File

Name: Arctic cod

Size: 20 to 30 centimetres

Appearance: Long, thin, brown body with black spots

Home: The Arctic Sea

Food: Microscopic creatures called plankton, and the eggs and larvae of other creatures. Some large Arctic cod also eat other smaller Arctic cod …ugh!

Don't worry – this isn't the same kind of cod that we eat with chips!

QUIZ Salt changes the freezing ***** of water. Wat

Arctic cod have been found further north than any other species of fish. They usually live in water colder than 0 °C, right next to the ice. The antifreeze chemicals in their bodies stop them from being frozen alive. Even so, they're so cold that they don't have much energy and spend a lot of time keeping still just below the ice.

12… I think. Or 13… I can't be sure… it's *dark in there!*

FiSH eaR FaCT

You can tell how old an Arctic cod is by counting the rings in its ear bones! It's just like counting tree rings – each ring represents a year.

Eye Spy!

> The hatchetfish lives deep down at the bottom of the sea. It has enormous lenses in front of its eyes to help it to see in the dark!

Flashy Fish!

Deep down in the ocean, it gets very, very dark. Some fish can't see anything at all down there. They use their sense of smell to find their way around instead! Other fish, like the hatchetfish you have just seen, have huge eyes to help them to see in the dark. Some deep-sea fish have eyes that are 30 times more sensitive to light than human eyes!

The deep-sea spiny dogfish produces light from its own body. It lights up the ocean floor so it can see where it's going. The light comes from a chemical reaction in the fish's body.

FiSHY FaCT

Fish lights are usually greenish-blue, because that's the colour that can be seen the furthest through water.

Some lanternfish have a light near their tail. If they are in danger from another fish, they produce a quick, bright flash of light. While the other fish is dazzled and confused, the lanternfish escapes!

Lanternfish spend the day in the deep ocean, but come close to the surface at night in search of food.

Some types of shrimp can squirt glowing juice into the water to distract their enemies. While the fish is looking at the puddle of light, the shrimp makes a quick getaway!

Fact File

Name
Deep-sea anglerfish

Size
Depending on the species, between 3 centimetres and 1.5 metres

Appearance
Round body, a long thread attached to its forehead, and big sharp teeth

Home
In the deepest parts of the ocean

Food
Smaller fish

The deep-sea anglerfish has its light on the end of the long thread at the front of its head, like the bait on the end of a fishing rod.

QUIZ The ✱✱✱✱✱✱✱✱✱✱✱ has enormous eyes

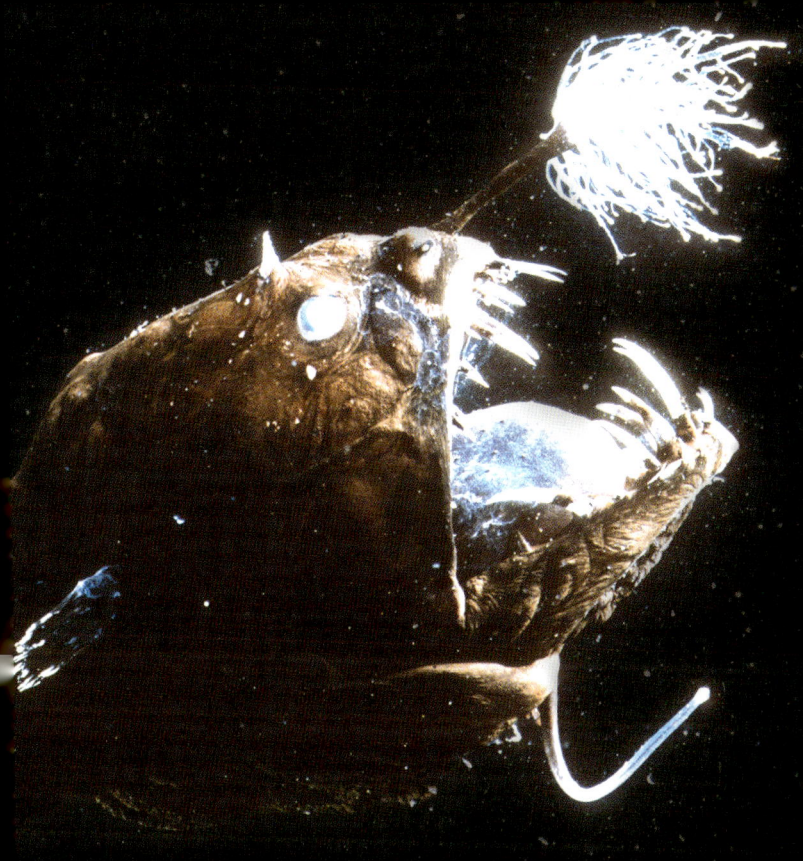

The deep-sea anglerfish flashes its light on and off to attract prey. Other creatures are attracted to the light and come closer to look at it. Then the anglerfish can easily snap them up!

Sunny Waters

The sunny, shallow waters of the tropical seas are warm and light, so lots of creatures can live there easily. Millions of microscopic creatures, called plankton, float about in the water. Plankton make good food for lots of other creatures, who don't even need to go hunting for them. There are so many plankton that other creatures just stay put and wait for the food to come to them!

Believe it or not, this 'flower' is actually a meat-eating creature!

Some of the most extraordinary sea creatures live in these warm, shallow seas … without even looking like creatures! Sea anemones look like flowers, but in fact they are meat-eating animals. They attach themselves to rocks and catch any passing plankton with a sticky substance on their long tentacles … or by stinging them!

Corals look like pretty rocks, or like plants that have turned to stone. But in fact they're meat-eating animals too! Corals are made up of lots of little creatures called polyps. The polyps have hard skeletons on the outside of their bodies, like a shell, and they all stick together in one big group.

As more and more polyps grow, they build up into big rock-like structures called coral reefs.

FeeDiNG FaCT

Corals may be animals, but they don't have a brain! Instead they have a network of nerves connecting their tentacles with their mouth.

Oi, stupid! Nah nah ne nah nah!

During the day, the polyps stay closed up, like a ball. At night, they open up and let their tentacles waft about in the sea. The tentacles sting or stick to any small passing creatures, and push them into the polyp's mouth. Some polyps can share the food they catch with the rest of the polyps in their group, because all their stomachs are connected!

Fact File

Name
Sea cucumber

Size
From a few centimetres up to about two metres

Home
On the sea floor, mostly in tropical, shallow waters

Appearance
Like a spiky cucumber! Some kinds are dull brown or green. Others are brightly coloured, with stripes and other patterns.

Food
Sucks up sand and eats the tiny creatures and particles of food found around the grains of sand.

The sea cucumber moves in short, jerky spurts by squeezing water out of its body. If it's really in trouble, it spews out its own insides, making a sticky white mess to put off the predator. Don't worry – its guts grow back again in just a few weeks!

QUIZ Sea cucumbers can grow up to two ★★★★

Some sea cucumbers can squirt out a very poisonous substance, which can kill all the fish nearby. This poison can harm human beings too … if you got it in your eye, it would blind you!

Sea cucumbers have hundreds of tiny feet with suction pads on them!

g. Sea anemones attach themselves to *****.

Ready to come up for air? On your dive, did you get all these answers to the quiz questions? Now, juggle with the first letters of all six answers to make a fishy word mentioned in this book.

Juggle the first letters SPHMR and you get SHRIMP – the only creature in this book you might like to eat!